W9-AQN-226

INNOVATORS

Shel Silverstein

Poet

Other titles in the Innovators series include:

INNOVATORS

Shel Silverstein

Poet

RACHEL LYNETTE

KIDHAVEN PRESS

An imprint of Thomson Gale, a part of The Thomson Corporation

THOMSON

™

GALE

Detroit • New York • San Francisco • San Diego • New Haven, Conn. • Waterville, Maine • London • Munich

LIBRARY OF CONGRESS CATALOGING-IN-PUBLICATION DATA

Lynette, Rachel.
    Shel Silverstein / by Rachel Lynette.
        p. cm. — (Inventors and creators)
    Includes bibliographical references and index.
    ISBN 0-7377-3555-4 (alk. paper)
    1. Silverstein, Shel—Juvenile literature. 2. Authors, American—20th century—Biography—Juvenile literature. 3. Children's stories—Authorship—Juvenile literature. I. Title. II. Series.
    PS3569.I47224Z765 2006
    818'.5409—dc22

                                                                2005032090

CONTENTS

CHAPTER 1

It Began with Cartoons

Poems by Shel Silverstein invite readers to imagine the impossible, giggle at the ridiculous, and think about the world in new ways. When Silverstein began writing for children, his poems and stories were unlike anything that had been published for children before.

Before Silverstein, most literature for children featured well-behaved characters, predictable plots, and happy endings. Silverstein thought that children should not be given role models who were impossible to live up to. The characters in his stories and poems often do things that adults do not like. They make mistakes and do silly and sometimes gross things. Silverstein wrote poems about eating babies, selling sisters, nose picking, lying, and a boy who literally loses his head. While some adults objected to his work, many shared their children's delight and fascination at Silverstein's humorous and insightful stories and poems.

Silverstein had a fascinating life and career. Before his death in 1999, he wrote and illustrated nine books for children as well

Shel Silverstein liked the characters in his stories
and poems to misbehave—just a little.

as many more for adults. In addition, he drew hundreds of cartoons, wrote and sang folk songs, wrote the musical scores for several movies, and was the author of many plays. He also traveled a lot and was always trying something new. In a 1975 interview with *Publisher's Weekly* he said, "I want to go everywhere, look at and listen to everything. You can go crazy with some of the wonderful stuff there is in life."[1]

Young Sheldon

Sheldon Allan Silverstein was born in Chicago on September 25, 1930, to parents Nathan and Helen Silverstein. He also had a younger sister named Peggy. Sheldon grew up in Logan Square, a neighborhood of mostly working-class families and immigrants.

Like many boys, Sheldon would rather play baseball than do his chores. He spent as much time as he could at the ballpark. Sheldon was a big White Sox fan and had dreams of someday joining the team. But by the time he was twelve, he realized that he was not a good enough athlete to ever make the team.

Since Sheldon could not excel at baseball, he turned his attention to drawing, another one of his favorite activities. As a teenager Sheldon wanted to attract girls. He thought being a good artist would make the girls in his school more interested in him. He told a reporter at *Publisher's Weekly* that "When I was a kid— 12, 14, around there—I would much rather have been a good baseball player or a hit with the girls. But I couldn't play ball, I couldn't dance. . . . So, I started to draw and to write."[2]

Sheldon did not take any drawing classes. Although there were several famous cartoonists in the 1940s and 1950s, he did not know about them. Instead of copying other people's work, he taught himself to draw. This allowed him to develop his own style of simple, bold lines.

Sheldon at School

Sheldon was known as a good artist but not as a good student. He did not follow directions well and was frequently in trouble with his teachers. He graduated from Roosevelt High School in 1947 and went on to attend the University of Illinois, where he planned to study art. But he continued to get bad grades and was asked to leave after only one year. He tried the Chicago Academy

Silverstein dreamed of playing baseball for the White Sox even though he was not very good at the game.

of Fine Arts next, but again he only lasted a year. Finally Silverstein wound up at Roosevelt University in Chicago, but this time he studied English.

Although his grades were poor at Roosevelt University, there were people there who realized that Silverstein was a talented artist and writer. One of these people was an English professor named Robert Coseby. Coseby liked Silverstein's work and encouraged him to continue to develop his talents. Later Silverstein would dedicate his first children's book to this teacher saying, "Even your old Uncle Shelby once had a teacher, His name was Robert Coseby. This book is dedicated to him."[3]

While at Roosevelt University, Silverstein began drawing cartoons for the monthly school paper, the *Torch*. His first cartoon

While a student at Roosevelt University (pictured), Silverstein was encouraged to develop his artistic talents.

was well received. Although he only drew five more for the paper, two of them were chosen for a collection of the *Torch's* best cartoons of the year.

In 1951 Silverstein began a column for the *Torch* called "The Garbage Man." In his column, he wrote about current events at the college and made jokes about his fellow students and professors. Silverstein enjoyed writing for the *Torch* and described his time there as exciting. The paper did not have a lot of money and often had difficulty paying its contributors. But the paper did have a lot of typewriters. At one point Silverstein received a typewriter as payment!

Silverstein was at Roosevelt for only three years. He did not graduate, because in 1953 he was **drafted** into the army to fight in the Korean War.

Army Life

Silverstein was on two military bases in the states before he was shipped off to Japan and then later to Korea. He was not a good soldier. He was frequently in trouble with his superior officers, although rarely for anything serious. For example, he once got in trouble for wearing socks with an argyle pattern with his uniform instead of the regulation army socks.

Although he was not much of a soldier, the military noticed Silverstein's artistic talent and assigned him to a job as a cartoonist and reporter for the military publication *Pacific Stars and Stripes*. His first comics made fun of officers in the military and of the military itself. Although they were generally good-natured and clever, not everyone appreciated his humor. While he was in the army, Silverstein compiled the comics he had done for *Pacific Stars and Stripes* into his first book. *Take Ten* was published in 1955. Later it was reissued as a paperback called *Grab Your Socks*.

**U.S. troops march past a line of fleeing Koreans.
Silverstein served in the army during the Korean War.**

Despite his poor performance as a soldier, and his knack for making fun of army life, Silverstein describes his experience in the army as a positive one. He got to travel and it gave him his first real job as a cartoonist. According to Silverstein, "It did me good, taught me things about life and gave me the freedom to create."[4]

CHAPTER 2

A Man of Many Talents

When Silverstein was discharged from the army, he had no idea he would someday be a famous children's writer. At that time his goal was to make his name in the world of cartoons. Although he had been a successful cartoonist in the army, he had trouble finding cartooning jobs once he was discharged.

Back in Chicago, Silverstein took a job at the Comiskey Park baseball stadium selling hot dogs and beer. Silverstein liked the job because he got to see a lot of baseball games. He was popular at the stadium and sold a record number of hot dogs! Silverstein also worked as a **freelance** cartoonist, occasionally selling cartoons to small publications. After a slow start, his career picked up in 1956.

Traveling the World

In 1956 Silverstein got his first real job as a cartoonist. He worked for a popular magazine. His first comics appeared in the magazine in March 1956. Within a few months, the editor of the magazine asked Silverstein to write a monthly travel column.

Silverstein sold hot dogs at Comiskey Park in Chicago while starting his career as a cartoonist.

This meant that he got to travel to places all over the world and write about them.

Silverstein spent several years traveling the globe. He went to many countries, including Switzerland, Italy, Russia, France, and Japan. The job ended in 1959 when Silverstein got into a bad car accident in Africa. His leg was shattered, and he was nearly killed. Silverstein returned home and decided to focus his talent in a different direction.

Shel the Songwriter

At home in America, Silverstein identified with the **counterculture** that was taking shape in the early 1960s. Some people (often known as hippies) wanted change. They did not believe that the

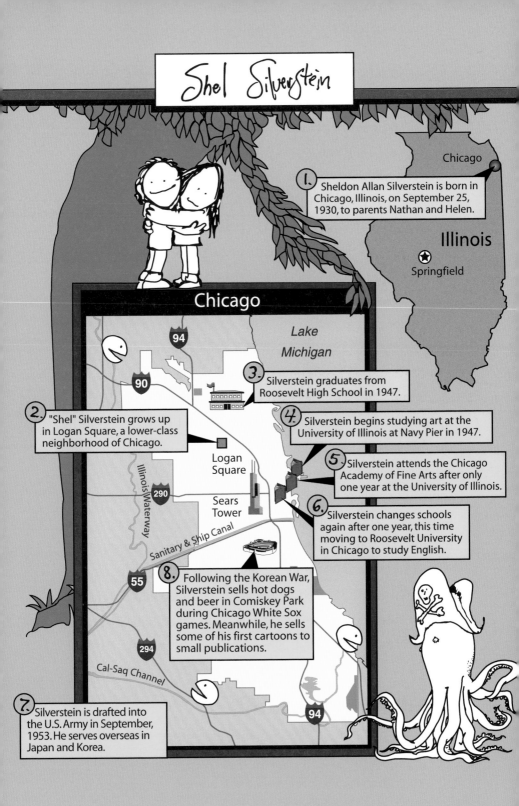

Shel Silverstein

1. Sheldon Allan Silverstein is born in Chicago, Illinois, on September 25, 1930, to parents Nathan and Helen.

Chicago

Illinois

Springfield

Chicago

Lake Michigan

94

90

3. Silverstein graduates from Roosevelt High School in 1947.

4. Silverstein begins studying art at the University of Illinois at Navy Pier in 1947.

2. "Shel" Silverstein grows up in Logan Square, a lower-class neighborhood of Chicago.

5. Silverstein attends the Chicago Academy of Fine Arts after only one year at the University of Illinois.

Logan Square

6. Silverstein changes schools again after one year, this time moving to Roosevelt University in Chicago to study English.

Sears Tower

Illinois Waterway

290

Sanitary & Ship Canal

8. Following the Korean War, Silverstein sells hot dogs and beer in Comiskey Park during Chicago White Sox games. Meanwhile, he sells some of his first cartoons to small publications.

55

294

Cal-Saq Channel

94

7. Silverstein is drafted into the U.S. Army in September, 1953. He serves overseas in Japan and Korea.

United States should be fighting in the Korean War. They believed that all people, including women and African Americans, should be treated equally. Silverstein embraced these beliefs. He often spoke about how people needed to be free to make their own choices. He was also active in the fight to **desegregate** America. He thought that black people should have the same rights as white people. Silverstein began to express some of these ideas through folk music, which was popular in the 1960s.

Silverstein had a raspy voice, but his songs were clever. People came to hear him sing in clubs. He released three albums of folk music in the 1960s. The first one did not sell well, but the second one, *Inside Folk Songs,* included "The Unicorn Song," a lighthearted song about how the unicorns were left behind when Noah built the Ark. The song was popular and was played frequently on the radio. Later the lyrics would be included in his first book of children's poetry, *Where the Sidewalk Ends.*

Silverstein made many friends in the music business, and soon other singers began to record songs that he had written. The most well known of these songs was "A Boy Named Sue," recorded by country singer Johnny Cash. The song is about a boy who is angry with his father for giving him a girl's name, because he is always being teased and beat up by other kids. Eventually the boy finds out that his father did it to make him tough. The song became a top-ten hit. Silverstein enjoyed more commercial success from this song than he ever had before.

Tender Young Minds

Even though he found success in songwriting, Silverstein was never happy to do just one thing. While he was singing and writing songs, he also continued to draw comics for magazines. In addition, he had written another humorous book. *Uncle Shelby's ABZ Book for Tender Young Minds* was made to look like a children's alphabet book. But it was actually a very funny book of different ways that children could get themselves and their parents into big trouble.

Country singer Johnny Cash recorded Silverstein's song "A Boy Named Sue."

Among other things, the book suggested that it would be fun to throw eggs at the ceiling, give daddy a haircut while he is sleeping, and break the TV with a hammer. It was marketed as a book for adults because the publishers worried that if children read it, they would not realize that the suggestions were jokes. As it turned out, children who read the book understood that it was not really an alphabet book. Although many readers thought the book was hilarious, Silverstein still did not see himself as a children's writer.

A First Book for Children

Tomi Ungerer, also an author and illustrator, realized that Silverstein's humor and quirky writing style would be appealing to children. He set up a meeting with his editor, Ursula Nordstrom, at her office in New York. Nordstrom, a well-known editor at Harper & Row Publishing, has edited many famous books that have since become children's **classics**. Although Nordstrom looked over Silverstein's cartoons at the meeting, she had been following his career for years and already admired his work. She agreed with Ungerer that Silverstein had something to offer to the

Author Tomi Ungerer, who wrote *Zeralda's Ogre*, encouraged Silverstein to write for children.

world of children's literature. He went back to Chicago and started writing.

Writing for children was an unexpected turn in Silverstein's career. According to Silverstein, "I never planned to write or draw for kids. It was Tomi Ungerer, a friend of mine, who insisted . . . practically dragged me, kicking and screaming, into Ursula Nordstrom's office. And she convinced me that Tomi was right; I could do children's books."[5]

The Story of Lafcadio

Within a few months Silverstein had written and illustrated his first children's book, *Uncle Shelby's Story of Lafcadio, the Lion Who Shot Back*. The story begins in Silverstein's unique way: "Once there was a young lion and his name was—well, I don't really know what his name was because he lived in the jungle with a lot of other lions and if he did have a name it certainly wasn't a name like Joe or Ernie or anything like that."[6]

The book tells the story of Lafcadio, a young lion who learns to shoot a gun and ends up going to the city and joining the circus. He starts to act a lot like a human. When he eventually finds his way back to the jungle and meets up with his old lion friends, he does not know whether he is a hunter or a lion. The idea of a lion hanging out with people is silly, and the book is quite funny. But it also makes the reader think about what it means to be human and that everyone does not live happily ever after. *Uncle Shelby's Story of Lafcadio, the Lion Who Shot Back* was published in 1963. Although it was not a runaway best seller, it did enjoy a moderate degree of success.

Silverstein illustrated the book with simple, yet bold line drawings. His black-and-white one-dimensional drawings were

**Silly stories and funny drawings formed the
heart of Silverstein's stories and poems.**

remarkably expressive and often humorous. He would use this same whimsical style to illustrate all of his works for children.

Silverstein's next book, *A Giraffe and a Half,* was a rhyming story written in the style of the classic children's poem "The House that Jack Built." Children enjoyed the silly story and illustrations. Critics praised Silverstein for his clever twist on a traditional poem.

By 1964 Silverstein was well on his way to making a name for himself as a children's author and illustrator. People were starting to appreciate the unique ideas and humorous writing style that would soon make him famous.

CHAPTER 3

Breaking New Ground

Silverstein's books for children were different from other children's books, because he believed that stories with easy solutions and happy characters were untruthful. He thought that when children read these stories, they would wonder why they were not as happy as the characters in the books or would feel like failures for not being able to find such easy answers to their own real-life problems. He wanted to tell children the truth in ways that they would understand. So he used humor, rhymes, and fablelike stories to present adult ideas.

Silverstein's unusual approach to children's writing often resulted in **controversy**. Some adults thought Silverstein's poems and stories were not suitable for children. They tried to have some of his books banned in schools and libraries, and in several places they succeeded. His books also caught the attention of book critics, college professors, psychologists, activists, and religious leaders. Countless essays, sermons, and reviews have been written about his books, starting with *The Giving Tree,* which was published in 1964.

The Giving Tree

The Giving Tree is the story of a tree that loves a boy so much that throughout the boy's life she gives him everything she has. At first, when the boy is young, she gives him shade and companionship.

Children and parents celebrate Silverstein's poetry during a reading. Some adults believed his poems were not suitable for children.

Musician Peter Frampton reads Silverstein's
popular book, *The Giving Tree*, to a packed
audience in 2004.

But as the boy grows, she sacrifices more of herself. She gives him apples, branches, and eventually, her trunk. The boy gives nothing in return. In fact he spends most of his life away from the tree, returning only when he wants something. At the end of the story, the boy is old and tired and only wants a place to rest, which she can provide since all that is left of her is a stump.

Silverstein told the story in simple, straightforward language with no rhymes and not a trace of humor. It was illustrated with Silverstein's now well-known simple line drawings. Silverstein sent the manuscript to several publishers, but no one wanted to publish *The Giving Tree*. Publishers felt the story was too sad for children and too simple for adults. Ursula Nordstrom (who had moved to HarperCollins) eventually agreed to publish it, but she was not comfortable with the project.

At first the book did not sell well. But gradually sales improved. After a few years, sales reached phenomenal heights. The book made the best-seller list, where it stayed for ten years! Today *The Giving Tree* is still widely read and considered a children's classic.

A Touching Story

The Giving Tree, read by many adults, has been interpreted in several different ways. A variety of people were touched by the tree's generosity. Some saw it as an example of unconditional love— perhaps the love of a mother for her child. Christians compared the tree's unselfish love to God's love for humans. **Environmentalists** believed the boy represented all of humanity and the tree represented the Earth. They thought the story was about how people have destroyed the resources of the Earth to meet their own needs. Some people thought the tree was stupid or crazy to give so much to someone who does not return her love. **Feminists** felt that by making the tree female, Silverstein was supporting the idea that women should give everything they have to others. Silverstein himself had very little to say about what he meant when he wrote the book, saying only, "It is just a relationship between two people; one gives and the other takes."[7]

The Giving Tree took people by surprise because of its serious nature. People may have worried that the silly, quirky Silverstein was gone forever. They had nothing to fear. In 1974 Silverstein published Where the Sidewalk Ends, a book of poems that delighted both children and adults.

A New Kind of Children's Poem

Suddenly children across America could not get enough poetry. Children not only read Silverstein's poems, they memorized them for fun and even wrote poems of their own. Parents and teachers were amazed. Never before had so many children reacted so positively to poetry. Never before had poems for children been written like the ones that Silverstein wrote.

Silverstein's first collection of poems, Where the Sidewalk Ends, contained 127 poems enhanced by Silverstein's unique illustrations. In 1981 he published a second collection, called A Light in the Attic. This book was longer, containing 263 poems, all of which were written especially for children. Both books sold millions of copies. Children loved the poems, and most adults did too.

Many of the poems in these books are silly. They feature kids who eat with their toes, wear toilet plungers for hats, and keep hot dogs for pets. Other poems are a mix of humor and horror. In "Fancy Dive" a woman does an elaborate dive only to realize too late that there is no water in the pool. The poem "Dreadful" is about how horrible it is that someone ate the baby. The "burp"

The Runner
Why does our track team run so fast
And jump with zest and zeal?
We owe it to our great coach
And our wonderful practice field.

~Shel Silverstein

Like many of Silverstein's poems, "The Runner" mixes humor with horror. One high school track team liked it so much they printed it on their sweatshirts.

in the last line lets the reader know exactly who the baby eater is. However, not all the poems are humorous.

Some of Silverstein's poems are touching and some are sad. "I Won't Hatch" is about a chick that refuses to hatch because he does not want to be part of a world where there is pollution and war. "Arrows" features a boy who shoots an arrow into the sky and accidentally kills a cloud.

Perhaps the most famous poem from these collections is "Sarah Cynthia Stout Would Not Take the Garbage Out," about a girl who let the garbage pile up until it reached the sky. Children love the grisly details of the garbage: "Brown bananas, rotten peas/Chunks of sour cottage cheese."[8] Parents like the lesson about how important it is to take out the garbage. But not every poem was popular with adults.

Some adults thought that Silverstein's poems encouraged bad behavior. In "Union for Children's Rights," children go on strike and demand things like shorter school days and higher allowances. In "How Not to Have to Dry the Dishes," the author suggests that children who drop dishes on the floor will not have to dry them anymore. Poems like these upset some parents and teachers. This resulted in both books being banned from schools and libraries in several states.

The Missing Piece

Silverstein wrote two more picture books for children. *The Missing Piece,* published in 1976, is the story of a shape that looks like a pizza with a slice missing. The almost-circle is on a quest to find a piece that will fit into its empty space. It has many adventures and eventually finds the piece it is looking for. But the shape soon realizes that it was happier without it, and so it leaves the piece and goes off on its merry way.

In 1981 Silverstein published a sequel, *The Missing Piece Meets the Big O*. In this book the wedge-shaped Missing Piece is on a journey to find a place to fit. After trying unsuccessfully to fit into various shapes, the piece meets the Big O. The Big O is

Some adults felt that Shel Silverstein's stories encouraged young people to behave badly.

not missing a piece and is perfectly happy that way. Soon the Missing Piece learns to be happy alone, too.

Like much of Silverstein's other work, both of these books were controversial. Some adults thought the books were sending the message to children that it is better to remain single than to get married. Despite the controversy, the books were popular. Both books were best sellers and are still popular today.

People often asked Silverstein what he was trying to say in his writings for children. He rarely explained his work. In 1963 he told a reporter from *Aardvark* magazine, "Never explain what you do. It speaks for itself. You only muddle it by talking about it."[9]

CHAPTER 4

Living Life on His Own Terms

By 1981 Silverstein had published nine books for children as well as several others for adults. He was well known as a children's author and had won several awards for his books, including the *School Library Journal's* Best Books Award and the International Reading Association's Children's Choice Award.

Although he enjoyed writing for children, Silverstein was always looking for new challenges. In the 1980s and early 1990s, Silverstein left children's writing and became a playwright. He wrote over fifteen plays for adults. Most were one-act plays full of Silverstein's bizarre humor. They were performed at festivals and in theaters in Chicago as well as in other parts of the country. He also wrote the musical score for several movies including *Coal Miner's Daughter* and *Postcards from the Edge*.

A Simple Life

Although Silverstein's books, plays, and songs had made him plenty of money, he did not act like a wealthy celebrity. He never

Silverstein divided his time between New York (where this photograph was taken) and Massachusetts, Florida, and California.

owned a car. He dressed in old clothes, usually sandals, jeans, and a faded shirt. Friends have said that he looked more like a homeless person than a famous children's author. He often wrote in coffee shops, sometimes scribbling ideas on napkins or whatever scraps of paper he could find. When he was not writing, he was spending time with friends, walking along the beach, or hanging out at flea markets or in used record shops.

Silverstein used his money to travel and to buy several houses in different parts of the country. He had homes in Martha's Vineyard, Massachusetts; Greenwich Village in New York City; and Key West, Florida; and he had a houseboat in Sausalito, California.

Silverstein cherished his privacy and avoided the spotlight. He refused to appear on television. In 1975 he gave his last interview, telling the reporter at *Publisher's Weekly,* "I won't go on television

Silverstein owned several homes. He also had a houseboat in the town of Sausalito, California (pictured).

because who am I talking to? Johnny Carson? The camera? Twenty million people I can't see? Uh-uh. And I won't give any more interviews."[10] Although he had no interest in fame, he was generally kind to people who recognized him. He was also happy to autograph books for children, often with a personal cartoon.

Two children he especially adored were his own, Shoshanna and Matthew. Shoshanna was born in 1970. She lived with her mother, Susan Hastings. Although he did not live with his daughter, he did spend a lot of time with her. *A Light in the Attic* was dedicated to "Shanna." Sadly, Shoshanna died in 1982 when an artery in her brain burst unexpectedly. Friends say that Silverstein was devastated by his daughter's death. Silverstein's son, Matthew, was born in 1984. When Silverstein did finally return to writing for children with *Falling Up,* he dedicated the book to him.

Falling Up

Silverstein's third collection of poetry, *Falling Up,* was published in 1996. It contained 140 poems. Like all his works for children, he illustrated it with his whimsical line drawings. Just as in his earlier collections, most of the poems are humorous. Again, some of his poems challenge adult authority. "Remote-A-Dad" is about a remote control that allows a kid to control his father—even to the point of turning him off.

This time, adults were not offended by Silverstein's writing style. Times had changed, and there were many other authors whose works were far more controversial than Silverstein's. *Falling Up's* popularity made it clear that Silverstein's writing was not outdated. Parents who had read *Where the Sidewalk Ends* when they were children now had a new collection of poems to share with their own children.

Gone But Not Forgotten

Silverstein passed away while writing in bed just three years after *Falling Up* was published. He died of heart failure in his Key West home in May 1999 at the age of 68. His friends and family were surprised by his death, as he took good care of himself and seemed to be in excellent health.

Silverstein left behind an amazing **legacy**. To Matthew he left an estate worth over 20 million dollars. To millions of adults and children, he left a lifetime of work. Silverstein's cartoons, songs, plays, stories, and poems are still popular today.

A drawing from *Falling Up* is projected onto a screen. Silverstein died just three years after the book was published.

Silverstein was inducted into the Nashville Songwriters Hall of Fame in 2002.

Since his death Silverstein has received several honors, including being inducted into the Nashville Songwriters Hall of Fame in 2002. In addition, many of his works have been reissued. Some of his older albums that had been off the market for years were made available again. His most popular works for children, including *Where the Sidewalk Ends* and *The Giving Tree* have been reissued as special "Anniversary Editions." People all around the world have enjoyed his work, as his children's books have been translated into over twenty different languages. Since his death there has even been a CD with a collection of songs for children written by Silverstein, called *Underwater Land*. Silverstein's longtime friend, Pat Dailey, sings the songs. In 2005 Silverstein's fans got an unexpected and very welcome surprise: a brand-new book of poems.

A collection of songs written by Shel Silverstein was released on CD by Olympia Records after his death.

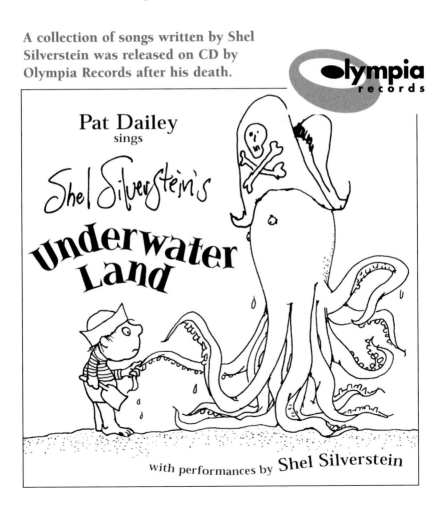

Runny Babbit

Silverstein had been working on *Runny Babbit: A Billy Sook* for over twenty years before his death. His nephew, Mitch Myers, compiled the poems and drawings for this new book. The book of 42 poems is different from his other poetry collections because the poems are full of **spoonerisms**. A spoonerism is a phrase in which the beginning sounds of two words are switched to make a funny sound or meaning. So, in the book's title, *Bunny Rabbit* becomes *Runny Babbit*

The poems in this book feature a cast of animals with spoonerism names: Runny Babbit, Toe Jurtle, Ploppy Sig, Rirty

Shel Silverstein hugs his longtime friend and singer Pat Dailey (right).

Dat, Pilly Belican, and many others. Even without the spooner-isms, the poems have Silverstein's quirky style and clever sur-prises. The book is popular with both children and adults. Children love the silly phrases: "Pea soup" becomes "sea poup," "ham sandwich" becomes "sam handwich." Parents and teachers like how sounding out the silly words helps children improve their phonics skills. Everyone seems to enjoy the challenge of mentally reversing the letters to find the meaning in the poem. *Runny Babbit* became a best seller soon after it was released and will most likely take its place beside Silverstein's other books of poetry as a classic in children's literature.

A Good Life

Silverstein was a gifted writer with a style all his own. He lived his life the way he wanted to and spent his time doing the things he loved. His many talents have enriched the lives of both chil-dren and adults. He told *Publisher's Weekly* "I would hope that people, no matter what age, would find something to identify with in my books, pick one up and experience a personal sense of discovery."[11] Silverstein's hope has become a reality; his work will continue to spark a sense of discovery in people for genera-tions to come.

Notes

Chapter One: It Began with Cartoons

1. Quoted in Jean Mercier, "Shel Silverstein," *Publisher's Weekly,* February 24, 1975, p. 50.
2. Quoted in Mercier, "Shel Silverstein," p. 50.
3. Shel Silverstein, *Uncle Shelby's Story of Lafcadio, the Lion Who Shot Back.* New York: HarperCollins, 1963.
4. Quoted in Hal Drake, "Cartoonist Silverstein Called *Stripes* His Catapult to Success," *Pacific Star and Stripes,* October 1, 1995. www.pstripes.com/pss50c.html.

Chapter Two: A Man of Many Talents

5. Quoted in Mercier, "Shel Silverstein," p. 50.
6. Silverstein, *Uncle Shelby's Story of Lafcadio, the Lion Who Shot Back.*

Chapter Three: Breaking New Ground

7. Quoted in Richard R. Lingman, "The Third Mr. Silverstein," *New York Times Book Review,* April 30, 1978, p. 57.
8. Shel Silverstein, *Where the Sidewalk Ends.* New York: Harper Collins, 1974, p. 70.
9. "Shel Silverstein: The Aardvark Interview," *Aardvark,* 1963. http://shelsilverstein.tripod.com/aardvarkl.html.

Chapter Four: Living Life on His Own Terms

10. Quoted in Mercier, "Shel Silverstein," p. 50.
11. Quoted in Mercier, "Shel Silverstein," p. 50.

GLOSSARY

classics: Works of art that are considered to be of high quality with lasting value.

controversy: A disagreement about a subject in which the participants have strong and opposing viewpoints.

counterculture: A group of people in a society who have ideas and ways of behaving that are intentionally very different from the values of other people in that society.

desegregate: To end laws or practices that permit different races to be restricted to separate public facilities, neighborhoods, schools, and organizations.

drafted: Ordered by law to join the military.

environmentalists: People who work to protect the natural world.

feminists: People who believe that women should have the same rights, power, and opportunities as men.

freelance: Working on short-term assignments for a variety of employers.

legacy: Something that is handed down from a previous generation or time.

spoonerisms: Reversals of the initial sounds in two words resulting in humorous phrases.

FOR FURTHER EXPLORATION

Books (Fiction)

Shel Silverstein, *Uncle Shelby's Story of Lafcadio, the Lion who Shot Back*. New York: HarperCollins, 1963. Silverstein's first book for children, is the story of a lion who learns to act like a human.

Shel Silverstein, *Who Wants a Cheap Rhinoceros?* New York: Macmillan, 1963. A silly book about the mischief that a rhinoceros can get into around the house.

Shel Silverstein, *Uncle Shelby's Giraffe and a Half*. New York: HarperCollins, 1964. This was Silverstein's second book for children. It is a story told in rhyme based on the style of "The House that Jack Built."

Shel Silverstein, *The Giving Tree*. New York: HarperCollins, 1964. A simple story about a tree who loved a boy so much that she gave him everything she had.

Shel Silverstein, *Where the Sidewalk Ends*. New York: HarperCollins, 1974. This is Silverstein's first collection of poems for children.

Shel Silverstein, *The Missing Piece*. New York: HarperCollins, 1976. In this book, a circle with a piece missing goes on a journey to find the missing piece.

Shel Silverstein, *The Missing Piece Meets the Big O*. New York: HarperCollins, 1981. In this sequel to *The Missing Piece,* the Missing Piece discovers how to be happy on its own.

Shel Silverstein, *A Light in the Attic* New York: HarperCollins,

1981. This is Silverstein's second book of poetry for children.

Shel Silverstein, *Falling Up.* New York: HarperCollins, 1996. A third collection of poems, this was the last of Silverstein's books for children published while he was alive.

Shel Silverstein, *Runny Babbit: A Billy Sook.* New York: Harper-Collins, 2005. Compiled by Silverstein's nephew and published six years after his death, this book of poems is full of silly spoonerisms.

Books (Nonfiction)

Cari Meister, *Shel Silverstein.* Edina, MI: ABDO, 2002. This short biography tells about Silverstein's life and career.

S. Ward, *Meet Shel Silverstein.* New York: Powerkids, 2001. This biography for younger readers features one-page chapters with pictures and samples of Silverstein's work.

Web Sites

Shel Silverstein: The Official Site for Kids (www.shel silverstein.com). This Web site features whimsical animations of Silverstein's illustrations as well as some interesting sound bites. There is also a short biography, kids' activities, and information about his works for children.

Shel Silverstein's Underwater Land (www.underwaterland. com). This is the Web site for the children's CD *Underwater Land* by Shel Silverstein and Pat Dailey. It includes biographies of the artists and sample selections that can be downloaded.

INDEX

PICTURE CREDITS

ABOUT THE AUTHOR

Rachel Lynette has written a dozen other books for KidHaven Press as well as many articles on children and family life. Rachel still has her copy of *Where the Sidewalk Ends* from her childhood and enjoyed sharing Silverstein's poems with her own children, David and Lucy. Rachel lives in the Seattle area, where she teaches science to children of all ages. When she is not writing or teaching, she enjoys spending time with her family and friends, traveling, reading, drawing, and inline skating.